Society Ethical Religion

Ethical Hymns

Society Ethical Religion

Ethical Hymns

ISBN/EAN: 9783744768108

Printed in Europe, USA, Canada, Australia, Japan

Cover: Foto ©Lupo / pixelio.de

More available books at **www.hansebooks.com**

ETHICAL HYMNS

SELECTED FOR THE USE OF

THE ETHICAL RELIGION SOCIETY

WITH PREFACE BY

W. R. WASHINGTON SULLIVAN

LONDON
SWAN SONNENSCHEIN & CO., Lim.
PATERNOSTER SQUARE
1899

ABERDEEN UNIVERSITY PRESS

PREFACE.

It may seem matter for surprise that they, whose ideal of "Worship" or "Divine Service" finds no place for vocal prayer, should continue to follow the ancient custom of singing hymns. But it will, I think, be readily recognised that the gradual transformation of "Divine Worship," from the extreme sacrificial rites of the Eastern and Latin Churches, where the priest is everything and the laity so many onlookers, to the deepening simplicity of pronounced Protestant communions, has led to a corresponding modification of the hymn as a factor in Religious Worship. The Christian hymn of the past was almost exclusively a pæan of praise to the Supreme Being or some hierarchical angel or saint, very much as ancient Greece and Rome sang chants in honour of Pallas Athene or Apollo. With the advent of the sixteenth century reform of religion, the adulatory poems to saints were discontinued, and henceforth confined to the celebration of the greatness and goodness of God, of His inscrutable Being and wonderful works, and to the glorifying of Jesus Christ. With the dawn of a still more searching reformation, which we may date from the era of Immanuel Kant, at the beginning of the present century, and which endeavours to recall men from the shadows that beguile them to the substance of things which is thereby obscured, the laudatory and supplicatory hymn is still further curtailed; in fact it undergoes an almost complete eclipse. A new genus of hymn appears calculated to more fitly express the new ideal of Worship, which has for its highest motive the kindling of an intense ethical enthusiasm in the hearts of its votaries.

Such a hymn is exactly adapted to Emerson's conception of a Religious Service, which is not an ecclesiastical function or a methodical series of ritualistic acts, and still less an atonement or propitiation of an offended Divinity, but an assemblage of men who meet "to encourage each other to good living". Such a service is held, not on behalf of the Deity, who needs nothing, but on behalf of humanity, which needs everything; and it is in a spirit of the most profound reverence that we make such a protestation.

Accepting this ideal of the legitimate expression of the religious emotion, believing that we best fulfil the Divine law of life by the dutiful observance of those spiritual laws of conduct which are to man what the physical laws are to inorganic nature, we sing such hymns at our services as we deem best calculated to awaken and sustain that ethical and spiritual fervour which is the only real source of well-being and well-doing, for individuals as for the community. Our idea is that life itself and its several duties are something sacred, that man has no need of church, priest or rite whereby to enter into the Holy of Holies, that he is ever in it, that—

> Our common daily life's divine,
> And every land a Palestine.

We endeavour to invest the conception of Duty, of which even the most heedless have some sense, with all those attributes of sanctity and solemnity hitherto associated with things remoter from human experience, and thus to give expression to our conviction that Religion *is* Morality and Morality *is* Religion, considered as a Divinely ordained law of life for all intelligent beings.

As a stimulus towards the adoption of the moral life, as a rebuke of the selfish, self-centred, unspiritual character for which " Faith " is no remedy, it is believed that hymns such as Whittier's are of incomparable value. For such purposes we retain them, for such purposes we sing them, that amid the sound of many voices and the strains of music their winged words may find entrance into the sanctuary of our souls.

The thanks of the Ethical Religion Society are gratefully given to Mrs. Bridell-Fox for her permission to use the hymns composed by the late W. J. Fox and Sarah F. Adams; to Messrs. Macmillan and Messrs. Chapman & Hall for verses published by them; to

Mrs. Bullock for verses by the late Dean Alford; to Lady Bowring for Sir John Bowring's lines; to Mrs. Clough for the late A. H. Clough's poem; to Mrs. Matthew Arnold for the late Matthew Arnold's verses; to Mr. Malcolm Quin for hymns 14 and 49, and to other owners of copyright for their courtesy in granting the use of the poems which stand part of the collection.

ETHICAL HYMNS.

1.

As once, upon Athenian ground,
Shrines, statues, temples, all around,
    The man of Tarsus trod,—
'Midst idol-altars, one he saw
That filled his breast with sacred awe:
    'Twas—" To the Unknown God ".

Age after age has rolled away,
Altars and thrones have felt decay,
    Sages and saints have risen;
And, like a giant roused from sleep,
Man has explored the pathless deep,
    And lightnings snatched from heaven.

Yet still, where'er presumptuous man
His Maker's essence strives to scan,
    And lifts his feeble hands,
Though saint and sage their powers unite
To fathom that abyss of light,
    Ah! still that altar stands.

A. L. Barbauld.

2.

"Make us a god," said man :
  Power first the voice obeyed :
And soon a monstrous form
  Its worshippers dismayed ;
Uncouth and huge, by nations rude adored,
With savage rites and sacrifice abhorred.

"Make us a god," said man :
  Art next the voice obeyed ;
Lovely, serene and grand,
  Uprose the Athenian maid ;
The perfect statue Greece, with wreathèd brows,
Adores in festal rites and lyric vows.

"Make us a god," said man :
  Religion followed Art,
And answered, "Look within ;
  God is in thine own heart—
His noblest image there, and holiest shrine,
Silent revere, and be thyself divine".

W. J. Fox.

3.

God of ages and of nations,
  Every race and every time
Hath received Thine inspirations,
  Glimpses of Thy truth sublime!

Ever spirits in rapt vision
  Passed the heavenly veil within,
Ever hearts bowed in contrition
  Found salvation from their sin.

Reason's noble aspiration
  Truth in glowing clearness saw;
Conscience spoke its condemnation,
  Or proclaimed the eternal law.

That which came to ancient sages,
  Greek, Barbarian, Roman, Jew,
Written in the heart's deep pages,
  Shines to-day for ever new!

Samuel Longfellow.

4.

Canst thou by searching find out God,
　　The Almighty to perfection trace?
And pierce the clouds when darkness shrouds
　　The brightness of the Eternal's face.

Go count the stars and call their names,
　　Sweep with the comet through the sky;
Fix thy bold gaze on the sun's blaze,
　　With an undazzled, tearless eye;

Go sleep upon the thunder cloud;
　　Grasp the forked lightning in thy hand;
Or search and find whence comes the wind,
　　And trace its path o'er sea and land.

Should thy mind shrink from such attempts,
　　View the least work of Deity;
The blades of grass thy skill surpass,
　　And thou art baffled by a fly!

No, every work of Nature's full
　　Of mysteries we can never scan:
Go thou—adore the Unsearchable,
　　Thou greatest of His mysteries—Man!

　　　　　　　　　　　From *Job* xi.

5.

Oh! I would sing a song of praise,
    Natural as the breeze
That stirs amongst the forest-trees,
     Whispering ever,
     Weary never,
Summer's prime or wintry days—
So should come my song of praise.

Oh! I would sing a song of praise,
    Sweet as breathing flowers
That ope to greet the earlier hours;
     Never-ending
     Incense sending
Up, to bless their parent rays—
So should wake my song of praise.

Oh! I would sing a song of praise,
    Holy as the night,
When heaven comes to us in the light
     Of stars, whose gleaming,
     Influence streaming,
Draws us upward while we gaze—
So should rise my song of praise.

S. F. Adams.

6.

LOOKING on Nature I have often felt
A presence that disturbs me with the joy
Of elevated thoughts; a sense sublime
Of something far more deeply interfused,
Whose dwelling is the light of setting suns,
And the round ocean, and the living air,
And the blue sky, and in the mind of man :—
A motion and a spirit that impels
All thinking things, all objects of all thought,
And rolls through all things.

Wordsworth.

7.

ALL are but parts of one stupendous whole,
Whose body Nature is, and God the soul ;
That changed through all, and yet in all the same,
Great in the earth as in the ethereal frame,
Warms in the sun, refreshes in the breeze,
Glows in the stars, and blossoms in the trees ;
Lives through all life, extends through all extent,
Spreads undivided, operates unspent :
To Him no high, no low, no great, no small ;
He fills, He bounds, connects, and equals all.

Pope.

8.

Diffused throughout infinitude of space
Who art Thyself thine own vast dwelling-place,
Soul of our soul, whom yet no sense of ours
Discerns, eluding our most active powers;—

Encircling shades attend Thine awful throne,
That veil Thy face, and keep Thee still unknown;
Unknown, though dwelling in our inmost part,
Lord of the thoughts and sovereign of the heart.

Mad. Guyon, tr. *Cowper.*

9.

When up to nightly skies we gaze,
Where stars pursue their endless ways,
We think we see from earth's low clod
The wide and shining home of God.

But, could we rise to moon or sun,
Or path where planets duly run,
Still heaven would spread above us far,
And earth remote would seem a star.

This earth, with all its dust and tears,
Is His, no less than yonder spheres;
And raindrops weak, and grains of sand,
Are stamped by His immediate hand.

The rock, the wave, the little flower,—
All fed by streams of living power
That spring from one Almighty will,—
Whate'er His thought conceives fulfil.

We view those halls of painted air,
And own Thy presence makes them fair;
But nearer still to Thee, O Lord,
Is he whose thoughts with thine accord.

Sterling.

10.

Music, divine, religious, o'er us roll!
Awake the longings of our inmost soul—
Longings that up to heaven itself would climb,
Extend beyond all space, outrun all time!
Thou only hast the power, denied to speech,
The vague, intense, ineffable, to reach!
Rise ever higher, wider swell, more wide,
Till, borne aloft on thy resistless tide,
We feel as though the harmony of heaven
Were part of us! Then, that high vision given,
Oh wake it not! but sweetly, gently cease;
And leave our heart with God and Man at peace!

H. K. Moore.

11.

All grows, says Doubt, all falls, decays and dies;
  There is no second life for flower or tree;
O suffering soul, be humble and be wise,
  Nor dream new worlds have any need of thee!

And yet, cries Hope, the world is deep and wide;
  And the full circle of our life expands,
Broad'ning and bright'ning, on an endless tide
  That ebbs and flows between these mystic lands.

Not endless life, but endless love I crave,
  The gladness and the calm of holier springs,
The hope that makes men resolute and brave,
  The joyful life in the great life of things.

The soul that loves and works will need no praise;
  But, fed with sunlight and with morning breath,
Will make our common days eternal days,
  And fearless greet the mild and gracious death.

W. M. W. Call.

12.

There is no wind but soweth seeds
    Of a more true and open life,
Which burst, unlooked for, into high-souled deeds
    With wayside beauty rife.

We find within these souls of ours
    Some wild germs of a higher birth,
Which in the poet's tropic heart bear flowers
    Whose fragrance fills the earth.

Within the hearts of all men lie
    These promises of wider bliss,
Which blossom into hopes that cannot die,
    In sunny hours like this.

All that hath been majestical
    In life or death, since time began,
Is native in the simple heart of all,
    The angel heart of man.

James Russell Lowell.

13.

Britain's first poet,
Famous old Chaucer,
Swan-like, in dying
   Sung his last song,
When at his heart-strings
   Death's hand was strong.

" From false crowds flying,
Dwell with soothfastness ;
Prize more than treasure
   Hearts true and brave ;
Truth to thine own heart
   Thy soul shall save.

" Trust not to fortune ;
Be not o'er meddling ;
Thankful receive thou
   Good which God gave ;
Truth to thine own heart
   Thy soul shall save."

Dead through long ages
Britain's first poet—
Still the monition
   Sounds from his grave ;
" Truth to thine own heart
   Thy soul shall save ".

A.

14.

Say not they die, those martyr souls
   Whose life is winged with purpose fine ;
Who leave us, pointing to the goals ;
   Who learn to conquer and resign.

Such cannot die ; they vanquish time,
   And fill the world with growing light,
Making the human life sublime
   With memories of their sacred might.

They cannot die whose lives are part
   Of that great life which is to be,
Whose hearts beat with the world's great heart,
   And throb with its high destiny.

Then mourn not those who, dying, gave
   A gift of greater light to man :
Death stands abashed before the brave ;
   They own a life he may not ban.

Malcolm Quin.

15.

The kings of old have shrine and tomb
In many a minster's haughty gloom;
And green, along the ocean side,
The mounds arise where heroes died;
But show me on thy flowery breast,
Earth! where thy nameless martyrs rest!

The thousands that, uncheered by praise,
Have made one offering of their days;
For truth, for heaven, for freedom's sake,
Resigned the bitter cup to take;
And silently in fearless faith
Bowing their noble souls to death:—

Where sleep they, Earth? by no proud stone
Their narrow couch of rest is known;
The still sad glory of their name
Hallows no fountain unto fame.
No—not a tree the record bears
Of their deep thoughts and lonely prayers.

Yet haply all around lie strew'd
The ashes of that multitude:
It may be that each day we tread
Where thus devoted hearts have bled;
And the young flowers our children sow,
Take root in holy dust below.

F. D. Hemans.

16.

CALL them from the dead
For our eyes to see!
Prophet-bards, whose awful word
Shook the earth, " Thus saith the Lord,"
And made the idols flee—
A glorious company!

Call them from the dead
For our eyes to see!
Sons of wisdom, song, and power,
Giving earth her richest dower,
And making nations free—
A glorious company!

Call them from the dead
For our eyes to see!
Forms of beauty, love, and grace,
"Sunshine in the shady place,"
That made it life to be—
A blessed company!

Call them from the dead—
Vain the call will be;
But the hand of death shall lay,
Like that of Christ, its healing clay
On eyes which then shall see
That glorious company!

W. J. Fox.

17.

Tell me not in mournful numbers,
  "Life is but an empty dream;"
For the soul is dead that slumbers,
  And things are not what they seem.

Life is real! life is earnest!
  And the grave is not its goal;
"Dust thou art, to dust returnest,"
  Was not spoken of the soul.

Lives of great men all remind us
  We can make our lives sublime;
And, departing, leave behind us
  Foot-prints on the sands of time.

Foot-prints that perhaps another,
  Sailing o'er life's solemn main,
Some forlorn and shipwrecked brother,
  Seeing, shall take heart again.

Let us then be up and doing,
  With a heart for any fate;
Still achieving, still pursuing,
  Learn to labour and to wait.

Longfellow.

18.

All are architects of fate,
    Working in these walls of Time;
Some with massive deed and great,
    Some with ornaments of rhyme.

Nothing useless is, or low,
    Each thing in its place is best;
And what seems but idle show
    Strengthens and supports the rest.

For the structure that we raise
    Time is with materials filled;
Our to-days and yesterdays
    Are the blocks with which we build.

Build to-day then strong and sure,
    With a firm and ample base;
And ascending and secure
    Shall to-morrow find its place.

Longfellow.

19.

When for me the silent oar
  Parts the silent river,
And I stand upon the shore
  Of the strange Forever,
Shall I miss the loved and known?
Shall I vainly seek mine own?

Can the bonds that make us here
  Know ourselves immortal,
Drop away like foliage sere
  At life's inner portal?
What is holiest below
Must for ever live and grow.

He who plants within our hearts
  All this deep affection,
Giving, when the form departs,
  Fadeless recollection,
Will but clasp the unbroken chain
Closer when we meet again.

Therefore dread I not to go
  O'er the silent river?
Death! thy hastening oar I know,
  Bear me, thou Life-giver,
Through the waters, to the shore
Where mine own have gone before.

Lucy Larcom.

20.

Once in the busy streets
  Did Wisdom cry aloud;
And then she perished, 'mid the scoffs
  Of the misguided crowd.

Once in the quiet grove
  Did Wisdom's accents charm;
And then she perished by the blows
  Of Conquest's iron arm.

In Palestine and Greece,
  Thus Wisdom's voice was hushed;
Yet Echo oft the sound renewed,
  Though Wisdom's sons were crushed.

But ever in the skies,
  In earth and sea and air,
Does Wisdom teach the human heart,
  And none can crush her there.

Systems and teachers change,
  They flourish and decay;
But ne'er from Nature's truth and love
  Shall Wisdom pass away.

W. J. Fox.

21.

The sage his cup of hemlock quaffed,
And calmly drained the fatal draught:
Such pledge did Grecian justice give
To one who taught them how to live.

The Christ, in piety assured,
The anguish of His cross endured:
Such pangs did Jewish zealots try
On Him who taught us how to die.

'Mid prison walls, the sage could trust
That men would grow more wise and just;
From Calvary's mount the Christ could see
The dawn of immortality.

Who know to live, and know to die,
Their souls are safe, their triumph nigh:
Power may oppress and priestcraft ban;
Justice and faith are God in man.

W. J. Fox.

22.

"Truth is great and must prevail!"
    Trite the adage: how and when?
Trial tells another tale,
    Truth has failed, will fail again
    If not backed by truthful men.

Truth is man's maturest thought,
    That the earnest grasp and try.
Who for truth has never fought,
    Who lets falsehood known go by,
    Propagates himself the lie.

Truth through deserts leads the way,
    Like a guiding fire from God,
Those who know its beam, and stray
    Far from where they're signed to plod,
    Keep the paths of truth untrod.

To the plough then lay your hand!
    Truth is nought when not embraced!
Look not back, nor listless stand
    Where your line of work is traced,
    Falsehood vanishes when faced!

Wisely said the Man of Love,
    "Who not gath'reth, scattereth!"
Truth's our mission from above,
    Work alone can show our faith,
    Help is life, indifference death!

A. J. Ellis.

23.

Thou long-disowned, reviled, oppressed,
    Strange friend of human kind,
Seeking through weary years a rest
    Within our hearts to find.

How late thy bright and awful brow
    Breaks through these clouds of sin !
Hail, Truth Divine, we know thee now,
    Angel of God, come in !

Come, though with purifying fire
    And desolating sword,
Thou of all nations the desire,
    Earth waits thy cleansing word.

Struck by the lightning of thy glance
    Let old oppressions die ;
Before thy cloudless countenance
    Let fear and falsehood fly.

Flood our dark life with golden day,
    Convince, subdue, enthrall ;
Then to a mightier yield thy sway
    And Love be all in all !

Eliza Scudder.

24.

Though wandering in a stranger-land,
Though on the waste no altar stand,
Take comfort! thou art not alone
While Faith hath marked thee for her own.

Would'st thou a temple? Look above,
The heavens stretch over all in love:
A book? For thine evangile scan
The wondrous history of man.

The holy band of saints renowned
Embrace thee, brother-like, around;
Their sufferings and their triumphs rise
In hymns immortal to the skies.

And though no organ-peal be heard,
In harmony the winds are stirred;
And there the morning stars upraise
Their ancient songs of deathless praise.

After Carlyle.

25.

The place of worship is not bound
   By arched roofs and stone-built walls,
Where prayers are said in endless round,
   As custom leads, or church bell calls.

Where solemn forms the truth encrust,
   The real hides beneath pretence;
And ages of tradition's dust,
   Still blind and choke the moral sense.

In flowery fields with bees and birds
   The heart may leap and join their hymn;
Worship is not confined to words
   In gloomy cells and cloisters dim.

'Tis where the hand with nature vies,
   And, ever working, blessing brings;
'Tis where the mind with reverence tries
   To find the mysteries of things.

The joyful heart is highest praise;
   Work, thought, and love, the loftiest prayer;
Where these are found, all times and days,
   The noblest place of worship's there.

Burrington.

26.

Fall, fall, ye ancient litanies and creeds;
    Not prayers or curses deep
    The power can longer keep,
That once ye held by filling human needs.

Fall, fall, ye mighty temples to the ground!
    Not in your sculptured rise
    Is the real exercise
Of human nature's brightest power found.

'Tis in the lofty hope, the daily toil,
    'Tis in the gifted line,
    In each far thought divine
That brings down heaven to light our common soil.

'Tis in the great, the lovely, and the true,
    'Tis in the generous thought
    Of all that man has wrought,
Of all that yet remains for man to do.

27.

One holy Church of God appears
    Through every age and race,
Unwasted by the lapse of years,
    Unchanged by changing place.

From oldest time, on farthest shores,
    Beneath the pine or palm,
One unseen Presence she adores,
    With silence or with psalm.

Her priests are all God's faithful sons,
    To serve the world raised up :
The pure in heart, her baptised ones ;
    Love, her communion cup.

The truth is her prophetic gift,
    The soul her sacred page ;
And feet on mercy's errand swift
    Do make her pilgrimage.

O living Church ! thine errand speed,
    Fulfil thy task sublime ;
With bread of life earth's hunger feed ;
    Redeem the evil time !

Samuel Longfellow.

28.

To light, that shines in stars and souls ;
    To law, that rounds the world with calm ;
To love, whose equal triumph rolls
    Thro' martyr's prayer and prophet's psalm ;
These walls are wed with unseen bands,
In holier shrines not built with hands.

May purer sacrament be here
    Than ever dwelt in rite or creed ;
Hallow'd the hour with vow sincere
    To serve the time's all-pressing need,
And rear, its heaving seas above,
Strongholds of freedom, folds of love.

Here be the wand'rer homeward led ;
    Here living streams in fulness flow ;
And ev'ry hung'ring soul be fed,
    That yearns the truer life to know,
And sow, 'mid patient toils and tears,
For harvests in serener years.

Samuel Johnson.

29.

Why thus longing, thus for ever sighing,
   For the far-off, unattained and dim ;
While the beautiful, all around thee lying,
   Offers up its low, perpetual hymn?

Wouldst thou listen to its gentle teaching,
   All thy restless yearnings it would still ;
Leaf and flower and laden bee are preaching,
   Thine own sphere, tho' humble, first to fill

Not by deeds that win the crowd's applauses
   Not by works that give thee world-renown
Not by martyrdom or vaunted crosses,
   Canst thou win and wear the immortal crown

Daily struggling, though unloved and lonely
   Every day a rich reward will give ;
Thou wilt find, by hearty striving only,
   And truly loving, thou canst truly live.
Harriet Winslow.

30.

Be true to every inmost thought ;
　　Be as thy thought, thy speech ;
What thou hast not by suffering bought,
　　Presume thou not to teach.

Woe, woe to him, on safety bent,
　　Who creeps to age from youth,
Failing to grasp his life's intent,
　　Because he fears the truth.

Show forth thy light ! If conscience gleam,
　　Cherish the rising glow :
The smallest spark may shed its beam
　　O'er thousand hearts below.

Face thou the wind ! Though safer seem
　　In shelter to abide ;
We were not made to sit and dream ;
　　The true must first be tried.

Alford.

31.

A NOBLER order yet shall be
   Than any that the world hath known,
When men obey, and yet are free,
   Are loved, and yet can stand alone.

Oh, boldly speak thy secret thought,
   And tell thy want, and by the wise
Be unto nobler action brought,
   And breathe the air of purer skies.

Strive less to bring the lofty down
   Than raise the low to be thy peers ;
Love is the only golden crown
   That will not tarnish with the years.

Soon the wild days of war shall end,
   And days of happier work begin,
When love and toil shall man befriend,
   And help to free the world from sin.
W. M. W. Call.

32.

Hast thou, 'midst life's empty noises,
　　Heard the solemn steps of time,
And the low mysterious voices
　　Of another clime?

Early hath life's mighty question
　　Thrilled within thy heart of youth,
With a deep and strong beseeching,—
　　What, and where is truth?

Not to ease and aimless quiet
　　Doth the inward answer tend,
But to works of love and duty,
　　As our beings end;

Earnest toil and strong endeavour
　　Of a spirit which within
Wrestles with familiar evil
　　And besetting sin;

And without, with tireless vigour,
　　Steady heart and purpose strong,
In the power of truth assaileth
　　Every form of wrong.

Whittier.

33.

All around us, fair with flowers,
   Fields of beauty sleeping lie;
All around us clarion voices
   Call to duty stern and high.

Following ev'ry voice of mercy
   With a trusting, loving heart,
Let us in life's earnest labour
   Still be sure to do our part.

Now, to-day, and not to-morrow,
   Let us work with all our might,
Lest the wretched faint and perish
   In the coming stormy night.

Now, to-day, and not to-morrow,
   Lest, before to-morrow's sun,
We too, mournfully departing,
   Shall have left our work undone.

34.

So here hath been dawning
   Another blue day :
Think, wilt thou let it
   Slip useless away ?

Out of eternity
   This new day is born ;
Into eternity
   At night will return.

Behold it aforetime
   No eye ever did ;
So soon it for ever
   From all eyes is hid.

So here hath been dawning
   Another blue day :
Think, wilt thou let it
   Slip useless away ?

Thomas Carlyle.

35.

O BROTHER man, fold to thy heart thy brother!
   Where pity dwells, the peace of God is there;
To worship rightly is to love each other,
   Each smile a hymn, each kindly deed a prayer.

Follow, with reverent steps, the great example
   Of Him whose holy work was doing good;
So shall the wide earth seem our Father's temple,
   Each loving life a psalm of gratitude.

Then shall all shackles fall; the stormy clangour
   Of wild war-music o'er the earth shall cease;
Love shall tread out the baleful fire of anger,
   And in its ashes plant the tree of peace.

Whittier.

36.

Oh, sweeter than the sweetest flower,
    At evening's dewy close,
The will, united with the power,
    To succour human woes.

And softer than the softest strain
    Of music to the ear,
The placid joy we give and gain
    By gratitude sincere.

True helpful kindness strikes a root
    That dies not nor decays,
And coming life shall yield the fruit
    Which blossoms now in praise.

The youthful hopes which now expand
    Their green and tender leaves,
Shall spread a plenty o'er the land
    In rich and yellow sheaves.

Drennan.

37.

Work! it is the highest mission,
    Work! all blessings centre there;
Work for culture, for the vision
    Of the true, and good, and fair.

'Tis of knowledge the condition,
    Opening still new fields beyond;
'Tis of thought the full fruition,
    'Tis of love the perfect bond.

Work! by labour comes th' unsealing
    Of the thoughts that in thee burn;
Comes in action the revealing
    Of the truths thou hast to learn.

Work! in helping loving union,
    With thy brethren of mankind;
With the foremost hold communion,
    Succour those who toil behind.

For true work can never perish;
    And thy followers in the way
For thy works thy name shall cherish—
    Work! while it is called to-day.

F. M. White.

38.

Ring out, wild bells, to the wild sky,
   The flying cloud, the frosty light :
   The year is dying in the night ;
Ring out, wild bells, and let him die.

Ring out the old, ring in the new ;
   Ring, happy bell, across the snow :
   The year is going, let him go ;
Ring out the false, ring in the true.

Ring out the grief that saps the mind
   For those that here we see no more ;
   Ring out the feud of rich and poor,
Ring in redress to all mankind.

Ring out a slowly dying cause,
   And ancient forms of party strife ;
   Ring in the nobler modes of life,
With sweeter manners, purer laws.

Ring out old shapes of foul disease,
   Ring out the narrowing lust of gold ;
   Ring out the thousand wars of old,
Ring in the thousand years of peace.

Ring in the valiant man and free,
   The larger heart, the kindlier hand ;
   Ring out the darkness of the land,
Ring in the Christ that is to be !

Tennyson.

39.

A VOICE by Jordan's shore,
  A summons stern and clear :
Reform ! Be just, and sin no more !
  God's judgment draweth near !

A voice by Galilee,
  A holier voice I hear :
Love God ! Thy neighbour love ! for see,
  God's mercy draweth near !

O voice of Duty, still
  Speak forth ; I hear with awe :
In thee I own the sovereign will,
  Obey the sovereign law.

Thou higher voice of Love,
  Yet speak thy word in me ;
Through duty let me upward move
  To thy pure liberty !

S. Johnson.

40.

He who has the truth, and keeps it,
    Keeps what not to him belongs,
But performs a selfish action
    That his fellow-mortal wrongs.

He who seeks the truth, and trembles
    At the dangers he must brave,
Is not fit to be a freeman,
    He at best is but a slave.

He who hears the truth and places
    Its high promptings under ban,
Loud may boast of all that's manly,
    But can never be a man.

Be thou like the noble ancient—
    Scorn the threat that bids thee fear;
Speak! no matter what betide thee;
    Let them strike, but make them hear.

Be thou like the first apostles—
    Be thou like heroic Paul;
If a free thought seek expression,
    Speak it boldly—speak it all!

Whittier.

41.

Oh, sometimes glimpses on my sight,
Through present wrong, th' eternal right;
And step by step since time began,
I see the steady gain of man:

That all of good the past hath had
Remains to make our own time glad;
Our common daily life divine,
And ev'ry land a Palestine;

For still the new transcends the old
In signs and tokens manifold;
Slaves rise up men, the olive waves
With roots deep set in battle-graves.

Through the harsh noises of our day,
A low sweet prelude finds its way:
Through clouds of doubt and creeds of fear
A light is breaking, calm and clear.

Whittier.

42.

Be perfect now and here,
  This be thy constant quest;
March boldly on, nor fear
  The high behest.

Though sins and frailties sore
  Thy higher manhood stain,
Cast them behind thee, nevermore
  To rise again.

Ask not forgiveness, then,
  But rather betterment;
Good men and angels surely so
  Shall be content.

Seek not to crush the powers
  That only training need;
But cherish, through the patient hours,
  The Godlike seed.

So, struggling up, shall strength
  Grow in thee on the way;
And doubt and darkness end at length
  In perfect day.

F. M. White.

43.

Hush the loud cannon's roar,
    The frantic warrior's call!
Why should the earth be drenched with gore?
    Are we not brothers all?

Want, from the wretch depart,
    Chains, from the captive fall!
Sweet Mercy, melt the oppressor's heart;
    Sufferers are brothers all.

Churches and sects, strike down
    Each mean partition-wall!
Let Love each harsher feeling drown;
    For men are brothers all.

Let Love and Truth alone
    Hold human hearts in thrall,
That Heaven its work at length may own,
    And men be brothers all.

Johns.

44.

Ye moments of eternal time
   That ever come and go,
And bear to ev'ry coast and clime
   Your freights of weal and woe;

Ye reap what former moments sowed,
   And, as ye onward sweep,
Drop in your course the seeds abroad
   Which after-moments reap.

And while ye singly troop along,
   Uncheck'd, relentless, fast,
Th' eternal spirit of your song
   Is future—present—past.

With eye of sense we only see
   The present moment's scope;
The past exists in memory,
   The future lives in hope.

Seize on the present, earnest mind!
   Call up your noblest pow'rs,
Dare to be swift,—we can but find
   The passing moment ours!

Frederick Burrington.

45.

Make channels for the streams of love,
   Where they may broadly run ;
And love has overflowing streams,
   To fill them every one.

But if at any time we cease
   Such channels to provide,
The very founts of love for us
   Will soon be parched and dried.

For we must share, if we would keep
   That blessing from above ;
Ceasing to give, we cease to have ;
   Such is the law of love.

Trench.

46.

WHAT is it that the crowd requite
  Thy love with hate, thy truth with lies?
And but to faith, and not to sight
  The walls of Freedom's temple rise?

Yet do thy work; it shall succeed
  In thine or in another's day;
And if denied the victor's meed,
  Thou shalt not lack the toiler's pay.

Faith shares the future's promise; Love's
  Self-offering is a triumph won;
And each good thought or action moves
  The dark world nearer to the sun.

Then faint not, falter not, nor plead
  Thy weakness; Truth itself is strong;
The lion's strength, the eagle's speed
  Are not alone vouchsafed to wrong.

Thy nature which through fire and flood,
  To peace again finds out its way,
Hath power to seek the highest good,
  And Duty's holiest cause obey!

Whittier.

47.

    Say not the law divine
Is hidden from thee, or afar removed;
    That law within would shine
If there its glorious light were sought and loved.

    Soar not on high,
Nor ask who thence shall bring it down to earth.
    That vaulted sky
Hath no such star, didst thou but know its worth.

    Nor launch thy bark
In search thereof upon a shoreless sea,
    Which has no ark—
No dove to bring this olive-branch to thee.

    Then do not roam
In search of that which wandering cannot win.
    At home! at home!
That word is placed thy very heart within.

Barton.

48.

All men are equal in their birth,
   Heirs of the earth and skies;
All men are equal when that earth
   Fades from their dying eyes.

'Tis man alone who difference sees
   And speaks of high and low,
And worships those, and tramples these,
   While the same path they go.

Oh, let man hasten to restore
   To all their rights of love;
In power and wealth exult no more,
   In wisdom lowly move.

Ye great, renounce your earth-born pride!
   Ye low, your shame and fear!
Live, as ye worship, side by side;
   Your brotherhood revere!

Harriet Martineau.

49.

Why repine we, why despair,
   Yielding to the instant woe?
We are not what once we were;
   Let us build on that we know.

Let the future and the past
   Make sublime the present hour:
What we do is doomed to last,
   And we know not all our power.

Even now the future life
   Shape we with unconscious hands;
Sudden, 'midst the woe and strife,
   Full our dream incarnate stands.

Lightest thought and humblest deed,
   Aspiration's faintest breath,
These are but the unseen seed
   That fructifies in spite of death.

Not despair, but wise devotion,
   Takes the meanness from our task;
High resolves and onward motion—
   These the passing moments ask.

Malcolm Quin.

50.

True worth is in being, not seeing—
　　In doing, each day that goes by,
Some little good—not in dreaming
　　Of great things to do by-and-bye.
For whatever men say in blindness,
　　And spite of the fancies of youth,
There's nothing so kingly as kindness,
　　And nothing so royal as truth.

We get back our mite as we measure—
　　We cannot do wrong and feel right,
Nor can we give pain and gain pleasure,
　　For justice avenges each slight.
The air for the wing of the sparrow,
　　The bush for the robin and wren,
But always the path that is narrow
　　And straight for the children of men.

51.

Heaven is here; where hymns of gladness
    Cheer the toiler's rugged way,
In this world where clouds of sadness
    Often change to night our day.

Heaven is here;—where misery lightened
    Of its heavy load is seen;
Where the face of sorrow, brightened
    By the deed of love, hath been;—

Where the bound, the poor, despairing,
    Are set free, supplied, and blest;
Where, in others' labours sharing,
    We can find our surest rest;—

Where we heed the voice of Duty
    Rather than man's wreath or rod;
This is heaven—its peace, its beauty,
    Tranquil with the peace of God.

J. Q. Adams.

52.

All before us lies the way;
  Give the past unto the wind :
All before us is the day;
  Night and darkness are behind.
Not where long past ages sleep
  Seek we Eden's golden trees;
In the future, folded deep,
  Are its mystic harmonies.

Eden with its angels bold,
  Trees and flow'rs and coolest sea,
Is less an ancient story told
  Than a glowing prophecy.
In the spirit's perfect air,
  In the passions tame and kind,
Innocence from selfish care,
  The true Eden shall we find.

It is coming, it shall come,
  To the patient and the striving;
To the quiet heart at home,
  Thinking wise and faithful living.
When the soul to sin hath died,
  True and beautiful and sound;
Then all earth is sanctified,
  Up springs paradise around.

Eliza T. Clapp.

53.

O PURE Reformers! not in vain
   Your trust in human kind;
The good which bloodshed could not gain,
   Your peaceful zeal shall find.

The truths ye urge are borne abroad
   By every wind and tide;
The voice of nature and of God
   Speaks out upon your side.

The weapons which your hands have found
   Are those which heaven hath wrought,
Light, Truth, and Love,—your battle-ground
   The free broad field of Thought.

O may no selfish purpose break
   The beauty of your plan,
Nor lie from throne or altar shake
   Your steady faith in man.

Whittier.

54.

Life is onward—use it
   With a forward aim ;
Toil is heavenly, choose it
   And its warfare claim.

Look not to another
   To perform your will,
Let not your own brother
   Keep your warm hand still.

Life is onward—heed it
   In each varied dress,
Your own act can speed it
   On to happiness.

His bright pinion o'er you,
   Time waves not in vain,
If Hope chants before you
   Her prophetic strain.

Life is onward—prize it,
   Sun-lit or in storm ;
Oh do not despise it
   In its humblest form !

55.

Live for something, be not idle;
    Look about thee for employ;
Sit not down to useless dreaming,
    Labour is the sweetest joy.
Folded hands are ever weary,
    Selfish hearts are never gay;
Life for thee hath many duties—
    Active be, then, while you may.

Scatter blessings in your pathway,—
    Gentle words and cheering smiles;
Better far than gold and silver
    Are their grief-dispelling wiles.
As the pleasant sunshine falleth
    Ever on the grateful earth,
So let sympathy and kindness
    Gladden well the darkened hearth.

Hearts that are oppressed and weary,
    Drop the tear of sympathy;
Whisper words of hope and comfort;
    Give, and thy reward shall be
Joy, unto thy soul returning
    From this perfect fountain-head;
Freely, as thou freely givest,
    Shall the grateful light be shed.

56.

Who is thy neighbour? He whom thou
  Hast power to aid or bless;
Whose aching heart or burning brow
  Thy soothing hand may press.

Thy neighbour? 'Tis the fainting poor,
  Whose eye with want is dim:
Oh, enter thou his humble door
  With aid and peace for him.

Thy neighbour? He who drinks the cup
  When sorrow drowns the brim;
With words of high sustaining hope
  Go thou and comfort him.

Thy neighbour? 'Tis the weary slave,
  Fettered in mind and limb;
He hath no hope this side the grave:
  Go thou and ransom him.

Thy neighbour? Pass no mourner by;
  Perhaps thou canst redeem
A breaking heart from misery;
  Go share thy lot with him.

Peabody.

57.

Ope, ope, my soul; around thee press
    A thousand things divine;
All glory and all holiness
    Are waiting to be thine.

Lie open; love and duty stand
    Thy guardian angels near,
To lead thee gently by the hand,—
    Their words of welcome hear.

Lie open, soul; the Beautiful,
    That all things doth embrace,
Shall ev'ry passion sweetly lull,
    And clothe thee in her grace.

Lie open, soul; the great and wise
    About thy portal throng;
The wealth of souls before thee lies,
    Their gifts to thee belong.

Lie open, soul; in watchfulness
    Each brighter glory win;
The universe thy heart shall bless
    And strength shall enter in.

Herbert New.

58.

There is in every human heart
Some not completely barren part,
Where seeds of love and truth might grow,
And flowers of gen'rous virtue blow;
To plant, to watch, to water there,
This be our duty, this our care.

And sweet it is the growth to trace
Of worth, of intellect, of grace,
In bosoms where our labours first
Bid the young seed of spring-time burst,
And lead it on from hour to hour
To ripen into perfect flow'r.

The heart of man's a soil which breeds
Or sweetest flow'rs or vilest weeds;
Flow'rs, lovely as the morning's light:
Weeds, deadly as the aconite:
Just as his heart is trained to bear
The poisonous weed or flow'ret fair.

Bowring.

59.

Have you heard the golden city
   Mentioned in the legends old?
Everlasting light shines o'er it,
   Wondrous tales of it are told;
Only righteous men and women
   Dwell within its gleaming wall,
Wrong is banished from its borders,
   Justice reigns supreme o'er all.

We are builders of that city,
   All our joys and all our groans
Help to rear its shining ramparts,
   All our lives are building stones;
But the work that we have builded,
   Oft with bleeding hands and tears,
And in error and in anguish,
   Will not perish with the years.

It will be, at last, made perfect,
   In the universal plan,
It will help to crown the labours
   Of the toiling hosts of man;
It will last and shine transfigured
   In the final reign of right,
It will merge into the splendours
   Of the City of the Light.

Felix Adler.

60.

Live thou thy life ; nor take thou heed
  Of shades or shapes of threatening ill ;
Walk thou where Nature's footsteps lead,
  And work in lowliness her will.

Let duty to thy soul be dear ;
  In doubt and weakness scorn to grope ;
Be steadfast, having nought to fear ;
  Be joyful, having much to hope.

What though the skies are dark to see,
  The ways are dim before thy feet :
If thine own soul be firm in thee,
  No harm there is that thou canst meet.

For courage treads a thornless road,
  While shadows fright the fearful soul ;
And hope will ease thee of thy load,
  And faith will bring thee to thy goal.

Live thou thy life, and ere it end
  Some grace acquire, some good bestow ;
When death shall come, thy final friend,
  Nor long to leave, nor fear to go.

Arthur Symons.

61.

How happy is he born and taught
    Who serveth not another's will—
Whose armour is his honest thought,
    And simple truth his only skill!

Whose passions not his masters are,
    Whose soul is still prepared for death,
Untied to this vain world by care
    Or public fame or private breath!

This man is freed from servile bands
    Of hope to rise, or fear to fall;
Lord of himself, though not of lands,
    And having nothing, yet hath all.

Sir Henry Wooton.

62.

Put forth thy leaf, thou lofty plane,
    East wind and frost are safely gone ;
With zephyr mild and balmy rain
    The summer comes serenely on.

Earth, air, and sun, and skies combine
    To promise all that's kind and fair,—
But thou, O human heart of mine!
    Be still, contain thyself, and bear.

December days were brief and chill,
    The winds of March were wild and drear,
And, nearing and receding still,
    Spring never would, we thought, be here.

The leaves that burst, the suns that shine,
    Had not the less their certain date :—
And thou, O human heart of mine!
    Be still, restrain thyself, and wait.

A. H. Clough.

63.

These things shall be! A loftier race
   Than e'er the world hath known, shall rise
With flower of freedom in their souls,
   And light of science in their eyes.

They shall be gentle, brave and strong,
   To spill no drop of blood, but dare
All that may plant man's lordship firm
   On earth, and fire, and sea, and air.

Nation with nation, land with land,
   Unarm'd shall live as comrades free;
In ev'ry heart and brain shall throb
   The pulse of one fraternity.

New hearts shall bloom of loftier mould,
   And mightier music thrill the skies,
And every life shall be a song,
   When all the earth is paradise.

These things—they are no dreams—shall be
   For happier men when we are gone:
Those golden days for them shall dawn,
   Transcending aught we gaze upon.

J. A. Symonds.

64.

I saw on earth another light
    Than that which lit my eye,
Come forth, as from my soul within,
    And from a higher sky.

Its beams still shone unclouded on
    When, in the distant west,
The sun I once had known had sunk
    For ever to his rest.

And on I walked,—though dark the night
    Nor rose his orb by day,—
As one to whom a surer guide
    Was pointing out the way.

Jones Very.

65.

Stern Daughter of the Voice of God!
    Oh Duty! if that name thou love,
Who art a light to guide, a rod
    To check the erring, and reprove;
Thou, who art victory and law,
When empty terrors overawe,
From vain temptations dost set free,
And calm'st the weary strife of frail humanity.

There are who ask not if thine eye
    Be on them; who in love and truth
Where no misgiving is, rely
    Upon the genial sense of youth;
Glad hearts without reproach or blot
Who do thy work and know it not:
Oh if through confidence misplaced
They fail, thy saving arms, dread Power, around them cast!

Stern Lawgiver! yet thou dost wear
    The Godhead's most benignant grace;
Nor know we anything so fair
    As is the smile upon thy face:
Flowers laugh before thee on their beds
And fragrance in thy footing treads;
Thou dost preserve the stars from wrong,
And the most ancient heavens through thee are fresh and strong.

Wordsworth.

66.

O RIGHTEOUS doom, that they who make
    Pleasure their only end,
Ord'ring the whole life for its sake,
    Miss that whereto they tend.

While they who bid stern duty lead,
    Content to follow, they,
Of duty only taking heed,
    Find pleasure by the way.

R. C. Trench.

67.

As o'er his furrowed fields, which lie
Beneath a coldly dropping sky,
Yet chill with winter's melted snow,
The husbandman goes forth to sow :

Thus, freedom ! on the bitter blast,
The ventures of thy seed we cast,
And trust to warmer sun and rain
To swell the germ and fill the grain.

It may not be our lot to wield
The sickle in the ripened field ;
Nor ours to hear, on summer eves,
The reaper's song among the sheaves :

Yet, where our duty's task is wrought
In unison with God's great thought,
The near and future blend in one,
And whatsoe'er is willed, is done.

Whittier.

68.

So should we live that every hour
May die as dies the natural flower,
A self-reviving thing of power;

That every thought and every deed
May hold within itself the seed
Of future good and future meed;

Esteeming sorrow, whose employ
Is to develop, not destroy,
Far better than a barren joy.

Houghton.

69.

The heart it hath its own estate;
    The mind it hath its wealth untold;
It needs not fortune to be great,
    While there's a coin surpassing gold.

No matter which way fortune leans,
    Wealth makes not happiness secure;
A little mind hath little means,
    A narrow heart is always poor.

'Tis not the house that honour makes,
    True honour is a thing divine;
It is the mind precedence takes,
    It is the spirit makes the shrine.

Swain.

70.

I hear it often in the dark,
    I hear it in the light,—
Where is the voice that comes to me
    With such a quiet night?
It seems but echo to my thought,
    And yet beyond the stars!
It seems a heart-beat in a bush,
    And yet the planet jars!

O may it be that far within
    My inmost soul there lies
A spirit sky that opens with
    Those voices of surprise.
Thy heaven is mine,—my very soul!
    Thy words are sweet and strong;
They fill my inward silences
    With music and with song.

They send me challenges to right,
    And loud rebuke my ill;
They ring my bells of victory;
    They breathe my " Peace be still ! "
They ever seem to say: " My child,
    Why seek me so all day?
Now journey inward to thyself,
    And listen by the way."

W. C. Gannett.

71.

Honour to him who freely gives,
    As Heav'n has blessed his store;
Who shares the gifts that he receives
    With those who need them more;
Whose melting heart of pity moves
    O'er sorrow and distress;
Of all his friends who mostly loves
    The poor and fatherless.

Honour to him who shuns to do
    An action mean or low;
Who will a nobler course pursue
    To stranger, friend or foe;
Who seeks for justice more than gain,
    Is merciful and kind;
Who will not cause a needless pain
    In body or in mind.

Honour to him who scorns to be
    To name or sect a slave;
Whose soul is, like the sunshine, free,
    Free as the ocean wave;
Who, when he sees oppression, wrong,
    Speaks out in thunder-tones;
Who feels that he with truth is strong,
    To grapple e'en with thrones.

72.

Born in each heart is impulse strong
   Aloft tow'rds heav'n its path to trace,
E'en as the lark its thrilling song
   Sings till all lost in azure space;

As eagle soaring sweeps amain
   O'er bleak untrodden pine-clad height,
As, struggling homeward still, the crane
   Urges o'er plain and marsh her flight.

Up, then, my soul, and never flag!
   Soaring the marsh of error past,
Thro' clouds of doubt, o'er trial's crag,
   Struggle to home in truth at last!

                      Suggested by *Goethe*.

73.

Go, my child, thus saith the highest,
   Warning, cheering, day by day,—
Go, my child, and as thou triest
   Life's temptations, bravely say:
   Do thy duty, 'tide what may!

Faint not! yield not! 'tis no sadness
   Burdens thee on life's true way:
Duty done is heartfelt gladness,
   Cheering as the summer ray:
   Do thy duty, 'tide what may!

When a cloud obscures the heaven,
   Know the sun will bring thee day:
When to grief thy soul is given,
   Trust that love will ever stay:
   Do thy duty, 'tide what may!

All the trials that surround thee
   Are but stones to mark thy way:
Nought will baffle or confound thee,
   Canst thou love, and bravely say:
   Do thy duty, 'tide what may!

A. J. Ellis.

74.

What conscience dictates to be done,
　Or warns me not to do,
This, teach me more than hell to shun,
　That, more than heaven pursue.

Let not this weak unknowing hand
　Presume thy bolts to throw,
And deal damnation round the land
　On each I judge thy foe.

If I am right, thy grace impart
　Still in the right to stay;
If I am wrong, oh, teach my heart
　To find that better way.

Save me alike from foolish pride,
　Or impious discontent,
At aught thy wisdom has denied,
　Or aught thy goodness lent.

Teach me to feel another's woe,
　To hide the fault I see;
The mercy I to others show,
　That mercy show to me.

Pope.

75.

The presence of perpetual change
   Is ever on the earth ;
To-day is only as the soil
   That gives to-morrow birth.

Where stood the tower, there grows the weed ;
   Where stood the weed, the tower ;
No present hour its likeness leaves
   To any future hour.

Of each imperial city, built
   Far on the Eastern plains,
A desert waste of tomb and sand
   Is all that now remains.

Our own fair city, filled with life,
   May have some future day
When power and might and majesty,
   Will all have passed away.

But in all changes brighter things
   And better may have birth ;
The presence of perpetual love
   Be ever on the earth.

Letitia E. Landon.

76.

Gently fall the evening shadows
   O'er the hills and o'er the plains,
Cattle slumber in the meadows,
   Hushed are now the wild birds' strains.

Whispering leaves in light winds quiver,
   Moonbeams flush the silent grove,
Stars gleam on the brimming river,
   Earth is wrapped in folds of love.

Have we in the day just going
   Breathed pure thoughts and purpose high,
Used the hours now past us flowing
   Wisely, ere the night draws nigh?

On our hearts sweet peace is falling
   Softly, like the shades of night,
And to each a voice is calling,
   " Be thou faithful to the right ".

Tozer.

77.

Men whose boast it is that ye
Come of fathers brave and free,—
If there breathe on earth a slave,
Are ye truly free and brave?
If ye do not feel the chain
When it works a brother's pain,
Are ye not base slaves indeed,
Slaves unworthy to be freed?

They are slaves who fear to speak
For the fallen and the weak:
They are slaves who will not choose
Hatred, scoffing and abuse,
Rather than in silence shrink
From the truth they needs must think:
They are slaves who dare not be
In the right with two or three.

Is true freedom but to break
Fetters for our own dear sake;
And, with leathern hearts, forget
That we owe mankind a debt?
No! true freedom is to share
All the chains our brothers wear,
And, with heart and hand, to be
Earnest to make others free.

Jas. Russell Lowell.

78.

A LITTLE child, in bulrush ark,
   Came floating on the Nile's broad water ;
That child made Egypt's glory dark,
   And freed his tribe from bonds and slaughter.

A little child inquiring stood
   In Israel's temple of its sages ;
That child, by lessons wise and good,
   Made pure the temple of past ages.

Mid worst oppressions, if remain
   Young hearts to freedom still aspiring,—
Though nursed in superstition's chain,
   If human minds be still inquiring,—

Then let not priest or tyrant dote
   On dreams of long the world commanding ;
The ark of Moses is afloat,
   And Christ is in the temple standing.

W. J. Fox.

79.

'Tis not by dreaming and delay,
    But doing something every day,
That wins the laurel and the bay,
    And crowns the work of duty.

Be satisfied that thou art right,
    And that thy deed will bear the light,
Then execute it with thy might,
    For that will be thy duty.

In nature's boundless universe,
    Thou wilt not see that dreadful curse,
An atom to its work averse,
    An idler shirking duty.

The planets as they roll on high,
    The river as it rusheth by,
For ever and for ever cry,
    "On, man, and do thy duty!"

All, all is working everywhere,
    In earth, in heaven, in sea, and air,
And nothing indolent is there
    To mar the perfect duty.

Edward Capern.

80.

How little of ourselves we know
    Before a grief the heart has felt!
The lessons that we learn of woe
    May brace the mind as well as melt.

The energies too stern for mirth,
    The reach of thought, the strength of will,
'Mid cloud and tempest have their birth,
    Through blight and blast their course fulfil.

And yet 'tis when it mourns and fears,
    The loaded spirit feels forgiven;
And through the mist of falling tears
    We catch the clearest glimpse of heaven.
Lord Morpeth.

81.

BEHOLD the way to God! the ascetic cries,
Fasting and prayer, a life of moans and sighs:
The world is dross, and all the world contains:
Heaven's crown is won alone by earthly pains!

Behold the way to God! the bigot cries,
Who dares to doubt for ever tortured lies:
Pray to the Lord and He will give you faith,
By scorn of life to triumph over death!

Behold the way to God! man's heart replies,
Hate is your hell and love your paradise:
Leave dreams to dreamers; do the best you can:
The way to God is through the heart of man!

A. J. Ellis.

82.

Happy they who are not weary
    Of this life's perpetual round,
Who at each fresh task and duty
    Feel their pow'rs in gladness bound;
Who are bent on winning knowledge,
    Bent on living true and high,
And on some good work achieving,
    Serving men, before they die.

Voices from behind, before us,
    From within and round us roll;
Firm to truth and love and loyal
    Be with lip and hand and soul;
O what triumphs are before you,
    As the years and ages move,
Error banish'd by true knowledge,
    Coldness by the breath of love;

Noble thought becoming freer,
    Uttered whole in word and deed,
Bigotry and thraldom dying,
    Of the state and of the creed;
Till of man a nobler pattern
    Sun and earth at length behold,
Broader-minded, broader-hearted,
    Tender, manly, reverent, bold.

T. W. Chignell.

83.

Speak gently!—it is better far
    To rule by love than fear;
Speak gently!—let no harsh word mar
    The good we may do here.

Speak gently to the young, for they
    Will have enough to bear;
Pass through this life as best they may,
    'Tis full of anxious care.

Speak gently to the aged one,
    Grieve not the careworn heart;
The sands of life are nearly run,
    Let them in peace depart.

Speak gently to the erring ones,
    They must have toiled in vain;
Perchance unkindness made them so,
    Oh! win them back again.

Speak gently!—'tis a little thing
    Dropped in the heart's deep well;
The good, the joy, that it may bring
    Eternity shall tell.

Haugford.

84.

What's hallowed ground? Has earth a clod
Its maker meant not should be trod
By man, the image of his God
    Erect and free,
Unscourged by superstition's rod
    To bow the knee?

Peace! Love! the cherubim that join
Their spread wings o'er devotion's shrine—
Prayers sound in vain, and temples shine,
    Where they are not :
The heart alone can make divine
    Religion's spot.

What's hallowed ground? 'Tis what gives birth
To sacred thoughts in souls of worth,
Peace! Independence! Truth! go forth
    Earth's compass round ;
And your high priesthood shall make earth
    All hallowed ground.

85.

There's a strife we all must wage,
    From life's entrance to its close ;
Blest the bold who dare engage,
    Woe for him who seeks repose.

Honoured they who firmly stand,
    While the conflict presses round ;
Duty's banner in their hand,
    In its service faithful found.

What our foes? Each thought impure ;
    Passions fierce that tear the soul ;
Every ill that we can cure ;
    Every crime we can control ;—

Every suffering which our hand
    Can with soothing care assuage ;
Every evil of our land ;
    Every error of our age.

86.

We see but dimly through the mists and vapours
   Amid these earthly damps ;
What seem to us but sad funereal tapers
   May be heaven's distant lamps.

And though at times, impetuous with emotion
   And anguish long suppressed,
The swelling heart heaves, moaning like the ocean
   That cannot be at rest,—

We will be patient, and assuage the feeling
   We may not wholly stay ;
By silence sanctifying, not concealing,
   The grief that must have way.

Longfellow.

87.

That man is great, and he alone,
Who serves a greatness not his own
    For neither praise nor pelf;
Content to know and be unknown,
    Whole in himself.

Strong is that man, he only strong,
To whose well-ordered will belong,
    For service and delight,
All powers that, in face of wrong,
    Establish right.

And free he is, and only he,
Who, from his tyrant passion free,
    By fortune undismayed,
Hath power upon himself to be
    By himself obeyed.

If such a man there be, where'er
Beneath the sun and moon he fare,
    He cannot fare amiss;
Great Nature hath him in her care,
    Her cause is his.

88.

The present, the present is all thou hast
    For thy sure possessing;
Like the patriarch's angel hold it fast
    Till it gives its blessing.

Like warp and woof all destinies
    Are woven fast,
Linked in sympathy like the keys
    Of an organ vast.

Pluck one thread, and the web ye mar;
    Break but one
Of a thousand keys, and the paining jar
    Through all will run.

O restless spirit! wherefore strain
    Beyond thy sphere?
Heaven and hell, with their joy and pain,
    Are now and here.

Back to thyself is measured well
    All thou hast given;
Thy neighbour's wrong is thy present hell,
    His bliss, thy heaven.

Whittier.

89.

Sweet is the pleasure
  Itself cannot spoil!
Is not true leisure
  One with true toil?
Thou that wouldst taste it,
  Still do thy best;
Use it, not waste it—
  Else 'tis no rest.

Wouldst behold beauty
  Near thee?—all around?
Only hath duty
  Such a sight found.
Rest is not quitting
  The busy career;
Rest is the fitting
  Of self to its sphere.

'Tis the brook's motion,
  Clear without strife,
Fleeing to ocean
  After its life.
Deeper devotion
  Nowhere hath knelt;
Fuller emotion
  Heart never felt.

J. S. Dwight.

90.

Sow in the morn thy seed,
   At eve hold not thine hand;
To doubt and fear give thou no heed,
   Broadcast it o'er the land.

Beside all waters sow,
   The highway furrows stock;
Cast it where thorns and thistles grow,
   Cast it upon the rock.

The good, the fruitful ground,
   Expect not here nor there;
O'er hill and dale by plots 'tis found;
   Go forth, then, everywhere.

And duly shall appear,
   In verdure, beauty, strength,
The tender blade, the stalk, the ear,
   And the full corn at length.

Thou canst not toil in vain—
   Light, heat and moisture, all
Shall foster and mature the grain,
   For harvest in the fall.

Montgomery.

91.

May all the good deeds of the past,
    And those that every day
Are done, without a selfish thought,
    Teach us the perfect way!

To live as faithful brothers live,
    In truly happy homes,
Where love is law, and no deceit
    Or doubting ever comes.

For thus to live is life indeed;
    To live not thus, is death;
All joy is hidden from the man,
    Who doubts with every breath.

There is an impulse in our hearts
    That makes for righteousness;
For trustful loving fellowship,
    For truth and faithfulness.

Then, O my brother, when in doubt,
    Let this thought give thee grace,
That in each heart however cold,
    Love hath a hiding-place.

And, O my soul, a blessing fair
    Thou shalt most surely prove,
If thou wilt fan the dying flame
    Of faith in human love.

F. W. Bockett.

92.

WEARY of myself, and sick of asking
    What I am, and what I ought to be,
At the vessel's prow I stand, which bears me
    Forwards, forwards, o'er the star-lit sea.

And a look of passionate desire
    O'er the sea and to the stars I send:
"Ye who from my childhood up have calmed me,
    Calm me, ah, compose me to the end!"

"Ah, once more," I cried, "ye stars, ye waters,
    On my heart your mighty charm renew;
Still, still let me, as I gaze upon you,
    Feel my soul becoming vast like you!"

From the intense, clear, star-sown vault of heaven,
    Over the lit sea's unquiet way,
In the rustling night-air came the answer:
    "Wouldst thou *be* as these are?—*Live* as they?

"Unaffrighted by the silence round them,
    Undistracted by the sights they see,
These demand not that the things without them
    Yield them love, amusement, sympathy.

"And with joy the stars perform their shining,
    And the sea its long moon-silvered roll.
Why? self-poised they live, nor pine with noting
    All the fever of some differing soul.

"Bounded by themselves, and unregardful
    In what state God's other works may be,
In their own tasks all their powers pouring,
    These attain the mighty life ye see."

Matthew Arnold.

93.

I cannot think of them as dead
   Who walk with me no more :
Along the path of life I tread
   They have but gone before.

And still their silent ministry
   Within my heart hath place,
As when on earth they walked with me
   And met me face to face.

Their lives are made for ever mine ;
   What they to me have been
Hath left henceforth its seal and sign
   Engraven deep within.

Mine are they by an ownership
   Nor time nor death can free ;
For Love hath given to Love to keep
   Her own eternally.

F. L. Hosmer.

94.

Part in peace! with rest before us
　Closing one more day of light;
Now—the shadows lengthening o'er us,
　Bless the care that guards the night.

Part in peace! with deep thanksgiving
　Rendering, as we homeward tread,
Gracious service to the living,
　Tender memory to the dead.

Part in peace! such are the praises
　That are meet for hours like this;
Such the worship that upraises
　Human hearts to heavenly bliss.

Part in peace! with deep thanksgiving
　Rendering, as we homeward tread,
Gracious service to the living,
　Tranquil memory to the dead.

S. F. Adams.

95.

What is the greatest good
   That this fair world can give?
What is the holy food
   On which our spirits live?
Which fills our mind with high desires
And all our noblest thought inspires?

What is the loftiest prize
   That we may strive to gain?
What vision fills our eyes
   With hope we may attain?
Which gives us courage to endure
And keeps our hearts and spirits pure?

Earth's greatest gift is love,
   And sweetest prize to win;
Treasure all else above,
   And source of life within.
O Love! Sweet Love! with us abide;
In life, in death, be thou our guide.

L. Rodd.

96.

There are lonely hearts to cherish
   While the days are going by ;
There are weary souls who perish
   While the days are going by ;
If a smile we can renew
As our journey we pursue,
Oh, the good we all can do
   While the days are going by !

There's no time for idle scorning
   While the days are going by ;
Be our faces like the morning
   While the days are going by :
Oh, the world is full of sighs,
Full of sad and weeping eyes ;
Help the fallen one to rise
   While the days are going by.

All the loving links that bind us
   While the days are going by,
One by one we leave behind us
   While the days are going by ;
But the seeds of good we sow,
Both in sun and shade will grow,
And will keep our hearts aglow
   While the days are going by.

97.

Once to every man and nation
   Comes the moment to decide,
In the strife of Truth with Falsehood,
   For the good or evil side ;

Some great cause, a new Messiah
   Offers each the bloom or blight,
And the choice goes by for ever,
   'Twixt that darkness and that light.

Then to side with Truth is noble,
   When we share her wretched crust,
Ere her cause bring fame and profit
   And 'tis prosperous to be just ;

Then it is the brave man chooses,
   While the coward stands aside,
Till the multitude make virtue
   Of the faith they had denied.

J. R. Lowell.

98.

For me—to have made one soul
   The better for my birth;
To have added but one flower
   To the garden of the earth:

To have struck one blow for truth
   In the daily fight with lies;
To have done one deed of right
   In the face of calumnies:

To have sown in the souls of men
   One thought that will not die;
To have been a link in the chain of life—
   Shall be immortality.

E. Hatch.

99.

Hours there will come of soulless night,
When all that's holy, all that's bright,
   Seems gone for aye :
When truth and love, and hope and peace,
All vanish into nothingness,
   And fade away.

Fear not the cloud that veils the skies,
'Tis out of darkness light must rise,
   As e'er of old :
The true, the good, the fair endure,
And thou, with eyes less dim, more pure,
   Shalt them behold.

Frederick M. White.

100.

O hallowed memories of the past,
    Ye legends old and fair,
Still be your light upon us cast,
    Your music on the air!
        In vain shall man deny,
           Or bid your mission cease,
        While stars yet prophesy
           Of love, and hope, and peace.

And while from out our dying dust,
    Light more than life doth stream,
We bless the faith that bids us trust
    The future that we dream.
        In death there is no fear,
           There's radiance through the gloom,
        While love and hope are here,
           The angels of the tomb.

Then, hallowed memories of the past,
    Or legends old and fair,
Still be your light upon us cast,
    Your music on the air!
        In vain shall man deny,
           Or bid your mission cease;
        The stars yet prophesy
           Of love, and hope, and peace.

S. F. Adams.

INDEX OF FIRST LINES.

	HYMN
A little child in bulrush ark	78
All are architects of Fate	18
All are but parts of one stupendous whole	7
All around us fair with flowers	33
All before us lies the way	52
All grows, says Doubt	11
All men are equal in their birth	48
A nobler order yet shall be	31
As o'er his furrowed fields	67
As once upon Athenian ground	1
A voice by Jordan's shore	39
Behold the way to God	81
Be perfect here and now	42
Be true to every inmost thought	30
Born in each heart	72
Britain's first poet	13
Call them from the dead	16
Canst thou by searching find out God	4
Diffused throughout infinitude of space	8
Fall, fall ye ancient litanies and creeds	26
For me to have made one soul	98
Gently fall the evening shadows	76
God of ages and of nations	3
Go, my child, thus saith the highest	73

INDEX OF FIRST LINES.

	HYMN
Happy they who are not weary	82
Hast thou midst life's empty noises	32
Have you heard the golden city	59
Heaven is here	51
He who has the truth and keeps it	40
Honour to him who freely gives	71
Hours there will come of soulless night	99
How happy is he born and taught	61
How little of ourselves we know	80
Hush the loud cannon's roar	7
I cannot think of them as dead	93
I hear it often in the dark	70
I saw on earth another light	64
Life is onward, use it	54
Live for something, be not idle	55
Live thou thy life; nor take thou heed	60
Looking on Nature I have often felt	6
Make channels for the streams of love	45
Make us a god, said man	2
May all the good deeds of the past	91
Men whose boast it is	77
Music, divine, religious, o'er us roll	10
O brother man fold to thy heart thy brother	35
O hallowed memories	100
Oh! I would sing a song of praise	5
Oh! sometimes glimpses on my sight	41
Oh! sweeter than the sweetest flower	36
Once in the busy street	20
Once to every man and nation	97
One holy Church of God	27
Ope, ope, my soul	57
O pure reformers, not in vain	53
O righteous doom	66

INDEX OF FIRST LINES.

	HYMN
Part in peace	94
Put forth thy leaf	62
Ring out, wild bells	38
Say not the law divine	47
Say not they die those martyr souls	14
So here hath been dawning	34
So should we live that every hour	68
Sow in the morn thy seed	90
Speak gently, it is better far	83
Stern daughter of the voice of God	65
Sweet is the pleasure	89
Tell me not in mournful numbers	17
That man is great, and he alone	87
The heart it hath its own estate	69
The kings of old have shrine and tomb	15
The place of worship is not bound	25
The presence of perpetual change	75
The present, the present is all thou hast	88
There are lonely hearts to cherish	96
There's a strife we all must wage	85
There is in every human heart	58
There is no wind but soweth seeds	12
The sage his cup of hemlock quaffed	21
These things shall be! A loftier race	63
Though wandering in a stranger-land	24
Thou long-disowned, reviled, oppressed	23
'Tis not by dreaming and delay	79
To light that shines in stars and souls	28
True worth is in being, not seeming	50
Truth is great and must prevail	22
Weary of myself, and sick of asking	92
We see but dimly through the mists	86

INDEX OF FIRST LINES.

	HYMN
What conscience dictates to be done	74
What's hallowed ground	84
What is it that the crowd requite	46
What is the greatest good	95
When for me the silent oar	19
When up to nightly skies we gaze	9
Who is thy neighbour	56
Why repine we, why despair	49
Why thus longing, thus for ever sighing	29
Work, it is thy highest mission	37
Ye moments of eternal time	44

INDEX OF AUTHORS.

	HYMN
Adams, J. Q. (1767-1848)	51
Adams, Sarah Flower (1805-1848)	5, 94, 100
Adler, Felix (*b.* 1851)	59
Alford, Dean (1810-1871)	30
Arnold, Matthew (1822-1888)	92
Barbauld, Anna Lætitia (1743-1825)	1
Barton, Bernard (1784-1849)	47
Bockett, F. W.	91
Bowring, Sir John (1792-1872)	58
Burrington, Frederick	25, 44
Call, W. M. W.	11, 31
Capern, Edward	79
Cary, Alice (1820-1871)	50
Carlyle, T. (1795-1881)	34
Chignell, T. W. (*b.* 1824)	82
Clapp, Eliza Thayer (1812-1888)	52
Clough, A. H. (1819-1861)	62
Cowper, William (1731-1800)	8
Drennan, William (1754-1820)	36
Dwight, J. S.	89
Ellis, A. J. (1814-1890)	22, 73, 81
Fox, W. J. (1786-1864)	2, 16, 20, 21, 78
Gannett, W. C. (*b.* 1840)	70
Goethe, J. W. von (1749-1832)	72
Hangford, G. W.	83
Hatch, Edwin (1835-1889)	98
Hemans, Felica (1793-1835)	15
Hosmer, F. L. (*b.* 1840)	93
Houghton, Lord (1809-1885)	68

INDEX OF AUTHORS.

	HYMN
Johns, John (1801-1847)	43
Johnson, Samuel (1822-1882)	28
Landon, Letitia (1802-1838)	75
Larcom, Lucy (1826-1893)	19
Longfellow, H. W. (1807-1882)	17, 18, 86
,, Samuel (1819-1892)	3, 27
Lowell, J. R. (1819-1891)	12, 77, 97
Martineau, Harriet (1802-1876)	48
Montgomery, James (1771-1854)	90
Moore, H. K. (b. 1846)	10
Morpeth, Lord (1802-1865)	80
Morris, Sir Lewis	13, 51, 78, 85
New, Herbert (1820-1893)	57
Peabody, W. B. (1799-1847)	56
Pope, Alexander (1688-1744)	74
Quin, Malcolm	14, 49
Rodd, L.	95
Scudder, Eliza (b. 1821)	23
Sterling, J. (1804-1844)	9
Swain, Charles (1803-1874)	69
Symonds, J. A. (1840-1893)	63
Symons, Arthur	60
Tennyson, Lord (1809-1892)	38
Tozer, E.	76
Trench, Archbishop (1807-1866)	45, 66
Very, Jones (1813-1880)	64
White, F. M.	37, 42, 99
Whittier, J. G. (1807-1892)	32, 35, 40, 41, 46, 53, 67, 88
Winslow, Harriet	29
Wooton, Sir Henry (1568-1639)	61
Wordsworth, William (1770-1850)	6, 65

www.ingramcontent.com/pod-product-compliance
Lightning Source LLC
Chambersburg PA
CBHW031402160426
43196CB00007B/856